For Cliff,

who gives me time to design.

THE CHARTS

Some of the designs in this book are very detailed and due to inevitable
space limitations, the charts may be shown on a comparatively small
scale; in such cases, readers may find it helpful to have the particular
chart with which they are currently working enlarged.

THREADS

The projects in this book were all stitched with Anchor stranded cotton
embroidery threads. The keys given with each chart also list thread
combinations for those who wish to use DMC or Madeira threads.
It should be pointed out that the shades produced by different
companies vary slightly, and it is not always possible to find
identical colours in a different range.

First published in 1996 by Merehurst Limited
Ferry House, 51-57 Lacy Road, Putney, London SW15 1PR
Copyright © 1996 Merehurst Limited
ISBN 1 85391 448 7

A catalogue record for this book is available from the British Library.

Edited by Diana Lodge
Designed by Maggie Aldred
Photography by Marie-Louise Avery
Illustrations by John Hutchinson and King & King (pages 22 and 26)
Typesetting by Dacorum Type & Print, Hemel Hempstead
Colour separation by Fotographics Limited, UK – Hong Kong
Printed in Hong Kong by Wing King Tong

*Merehurst is the leading publisher of craft books and has an excellent range
of titles to suit all levels. Please send to the address above for our
free catalogue, stating the title of this book.*

CONTENTS

$\mathscr{I}$NTRODUCTION

$\mathbf{H}$ere is a book that combines all the best-loved characters of the farmyard. The carefully-designed projects depict farm favourites which have been placed in settings that echo the richness of the countryside, and of rural life. Colourful and realistic, the animals really come to life on your fabric. Many of the designs are tastefully decorated with borders of wild flowers or country hedges to complement the colours of the animals within.

The projects offer scope for development of newly-acquired skills, or the chance to create a quick and easy idea for the complete beginner. Each project is beautifully illustrated with a full colour picture, accompanied by an easy-to-follow chart and full details for completing each of the cross stitch items.

The projects will enhance your home in a decorative sense, and for the more practically minded, they offer rewarding yet attractive ways to put your skill with the needle to good use.

Happy stitching!

$\mathscr{B}$ASIC SKILLS

∎

BEFORE YOU BEGIN

PREPARING THE FABRIC
Even with an average amount of handling, many evenweave fabrics tend to fray at the edges, so it is a good idea to overcast the raw edges, using ordinary sewing thread, before you begin.

FABRIC
Most of the projects in this book use 14-count Aida fabric, which has a surface of 14 clearly defined squares or 'blocks' of thread per 2.5cm (1in). Other fabrics used are 25-count Lugano, 27-count Linda and 22-count Anne; these fabrics are evenweaves, having the same number of warp and weft threads per 2.5cm (1in), and stitches are taken over two threads in each direction. All of these fabrics are produced by Zweigart.

THE INSTRUCTIONS
Each project begins with a full list of the materials that you will require. The measurements given for the embroidery fabric include a minimum of 5cm (2in) all around to allow for stretching it in a frame and preparing the edges to prevent them from fraying.

Colour keys for stranded embroidery cottons – Anchor, DMC, or Madeira – are given with each chart. It is assumed that you will need to buy one skein of each colour mentioned in a particular key, even though you may use less, but where two or more skeins are needed, this information is included in the main list of requirements.

Before you begin to embroider, always mark the centre of the design with two lines of basting stitches, one vertical and one horizontal, running from edge to edge of the fabric, as indicated by the arrows on the charts.

As you stitch, use the centre lines given on the chart and the basting threads on your fabric as reference points for counting the squares and threads to position your design accurately.

WORKING IN A HOOP

A hoop is the most popular frame for use with small areas of embroidery. It consists of two rings, one fitted inside the other; the outer ring usually has an adjustable screw attachment so that it can be tightened to hold the stretched fabric in place. Hoops are available in several sizes, ranging from 10cm (4in) in diameter to quilting hoops with a diameter of 38cm (15in). Hoops with table stands or floor stands attached are also available.

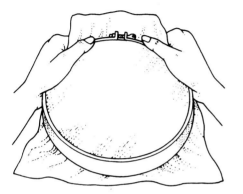

1 To stretch your fabric in a hoop, place the area to be embroidered over the inner ring and press the outer ring over it, with the tension screw released. Tissue paper can be placed between the outer ring and the embroidery, so that the hoop does not mark the fabric. Lay the tissue paper over the fabric when you set it in the hoop, then tear away the central embroidery area.

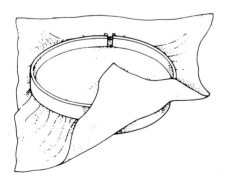

2 Smooth the fabric and, if necessary, straighten the grain before tightening the screw. The fabric should be evenly stretched.

WORKING IN A RECTANGULAR FRAME

Rectangular frames are more suitable for larger pieces of embroidery. They consist of two rollers, with tapes attached, and two flat side pieces, which slot into the rollers and are held in place by pegs or screw attachments. Available in different sizes, either alone or with adjustable table or floor stands, frames are measured by the length of the roller tape, and range in size from 30cm (12in) to 68cm (27in).

As alternatives to a slate frame, canvas stretchers and the backs of old picture frames can be used. Provided there is sufficient extra fabric around the finished size of the embroidery, the edges can be turned under and simply attached with drawing pins (thumb tacks) or staples.

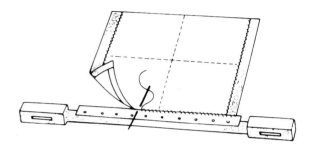

1 To stretch your fabric in a rectangular frame, cut out the fabric, allowing at least an extra 5cm (2in) all around the finished size of the embroidery. Baste a single 12mm (½in) turning on the top and bottom edges and oversew strong tape, 2.5cm (1in) wide, to the other two sides. Mark the centre line both ways with basting stitches. Working from the centre outward and using strong thread, oversew the top and bottom edges to the roller tapes. Fit the side pieces into the slots, and roll any extra fabric on one roller until the fabric is taut.

2 Insert the pegs or adjust the screw attachments to secure the frame. Thread a large-eyed needle (chenille needle) with strong thread or fine string and lace both edges, securing the ends around the intersections of the frame. Lace the webbing at 2.5cm (1in) intervals, stretching the fabric evenly.

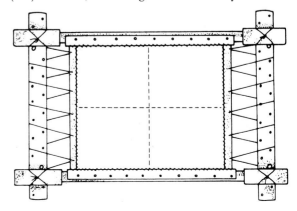

EXTENDING EMBROIDERY FABRIC

It is easy to extend a piece of embroidery fabric, such as a bookmark, to stretch it in a hoop.

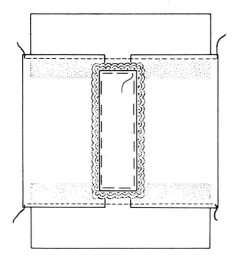

● Fabric oddments of a similar weight can be used. Simply cut four pieces to size (in other words, to the measurement that will fit both the embroidery fabric and your hoop) and baste them to each side of the embroidery fabric before stretching it in the hoop in the usual way.

THE STITCHES

CROSS STITCH

For all cross stitch embroidery, the following two methods of working are used. In each case, neat rows of vertical stitches are produced on the back of the fabric.

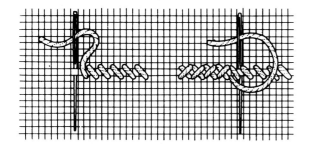

● When stitching large areas, work in horizontal rows. Working from right to left, complete the first row of evenly spaced diagonal stitches over the number of threads specified in the project instructions. Then, working from left to right, repeat the process. Continue in this way, making sure each stitch crosses in the same direction.

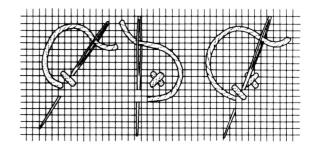

● When stitching diagonal lines, work downwards, completing each stitch before moving to the next. When starting a project always begin to embroider at the centre of the design and work outwards to ensure that the design will be placed centrally on the fabric.

BACKSTITCH

Backstitch is used in the projects to give emphasis to a particular foldline, an outline or a shadow. The stitches are worked over the same number of threads as the cross stitch, forming continuous straight or diagonal lines.

● Make the first stitch from left to right; pass the needle behind the fabric and bring it out one stitch length ahead to the left. Repeat and continue in this way along the line.

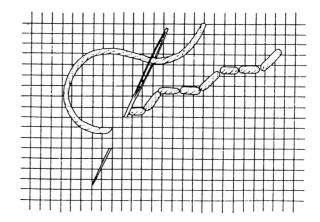

THREE-QUARTER CROSS STITCHES

Some fractional stitches are used on certain projects in this book; although they strike fear into the hearts of less experienced stitchers they are not difficult to master, and give a more natural line in certain instances. Should you find it difficult to pierce the centre of the Aida block, simply use a sharp needle to make a small hole in the centre first.

To work a three-quarter cross, bring the needle up

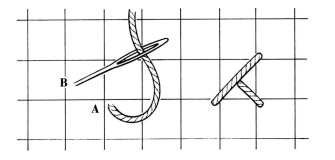

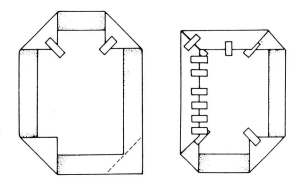

at point A and down through the centre of the square at B. Later, the diagonal back stitch finishes the stitch. A chart square with two different symbols separated by a diagonal line requires two 'three-quarter' stitches. Backstitch will later finish the square.

FRENCH KNOTS

This stitch is shown on some of the diagrams by a small circle. Where there are several french knots, the circles have been omitted to avoid confusion. Where this occurs you should refer to the instructions of the project, the detail chart and the colour photograph.

To work a french knot, bring your needle and cotton out slightly to the right of where you want your knot to be. Wind the thread once or twice around the needle, depending on how big you want your knot to be, and insert the needle to the left of the point where you brought it out.

Be careful not to pull too hard or the knot will disappear through the fabric. The instructions state the number of strands of cotton to be used for the french knots.

FINISHING

MOUNTING EMBROIDERY

The cardboard should be cut to the size of the finished embroidery, with an extra 6mm (¹⁄₄in) added all round to allow for the recess in the frame.

1 Place embroidery face down, with the cardboard centred on top, and basting and pencil lines matching. Begin by folding over the fabric at each corner and securing it with masking tape.

2 Working first on one side and then the other, fold over the fabric on all sides and secure it firmly with pieces of masking tape, placed about 2.5cm (1in) apart. Also neaten the mitred corners with masking tape, pulling the fabric tightly to give a firm, smooth finish.

HEAVIER FABRICS

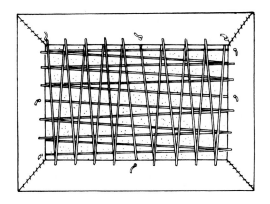

● Lay the embroidery face down, with the cardboard centred on top; fold over the edges of the fabric on opposite sides, making mitred folds at the corners, and lace across, using strong thread. Repeat on the other two sides. Finally, pull up the fabric firmly over the cardboard. Overstitch the mitred corners.

Plough
Horses

Plough horses are famous for their
gentle natures, and this picture of
a pair of plough horses at rest
combines strength and delicacy,
with the dark background bringing
the subtle shading of the horses
forward for a really dramatic effect.

PLOUGH HORSES

YOU WILL NEED

For the *Plough Horses* picture, with a design area measuring 18.5cm × 15.5cm (7¼ in × 6 in), here set in a frame with an internal measurement of 27.5cm × 29.5cm (10¾ in × 11¾ in):

34cm × 28cm (13½ in × 11in) of dark blue, 14-count Aida fabric
Stranded embroidery cotton in the colours given in the panel
No24 tapestry needle
Frame, as specified above
Strong thread and cardboard, for mounting

●

THE EMBROIDERY

Prepare the fabric as described on page 4; find the centre by folding, and mark the horizontal and vertical centre lines with basting stitches in a light-coloured thread. Set the fabric in a frame and count out from the centre to start stitching at a point convenient to you.

Complete the cross stitching, use two strands of thread in the needle for all colours except fawn, pale grey blue, cream, and very pale grey blue, which are stitched with three strands in the needle. Make sure that all top stitches run in the same direction.

FINISHING

Remove the embroidery from the frame. Gently handwash the finished piece, if necessary, and lightly press with a steam iron on the wrong side. Stretch and mount the embroidery as explained on page 6. Insert the mounted picture into the frame, and assemble the frame according to the manufacturer's instructions.

PLOUGH HORSES ▶	ANCHOR	DMC	MADEIRA
□ Fawn	388	3033	2001
+ Pale grey blue	848	927	1708
T Donkey brown	379	840	1912
⊢ Dark grey purple	233	451	1808
⊬ Pale blue	144	794	0907
▪ Sand	372	676	2208
⊔ Grey	399	414	1801
∷ Darker pink	894	224	0813
⊔ Grey brown	903	3790	2107
⊓ Gold	362	834	2204
· Cream	926	822	2101
⊠ Very pale grey blue	847	928	1709
⊠ Pale donkey brown	378	841	1911
■ Dark brown	380	839	1913
⊣ Pale grey purple	232	452	1807
⊤ Blue	145	793	0906
⊥ Dark sand	373	729	2209
– Pale pink	893	225	0814
⊤ Rich brown	358	433	2008
⊏ Stone	392	642	1906

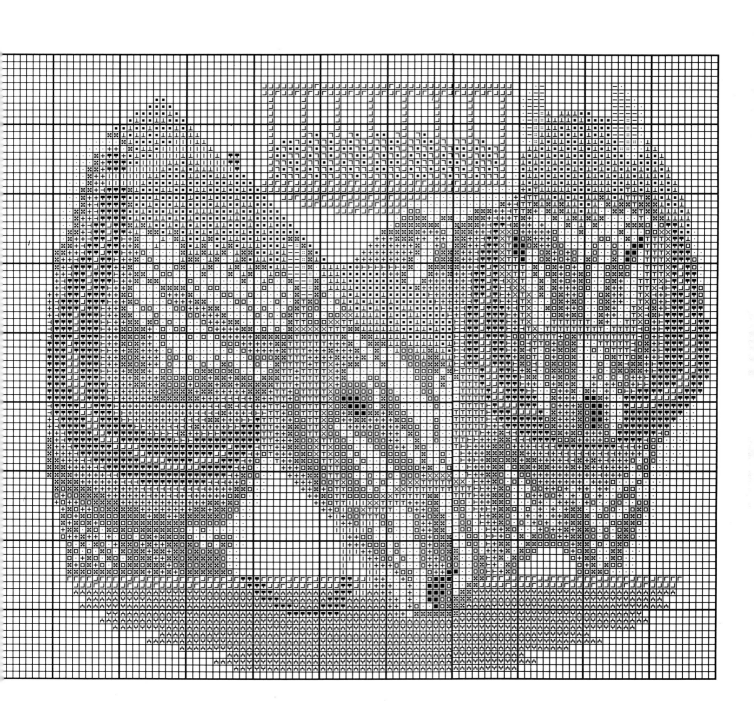

Cow and Calf Tray Cloth

The mother and her young baby in this charming study of a cow and calf are stitched in rich creamy browns and set in a formal border of bright cornflowers.

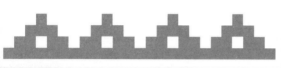

COW AND CALF
TRAY CLOTH

YOU WILL NEED

For the tray cloth, with a design area measuring 29cm × 22cm (11¹⁄₂in × 8³⁄₄in), on a tray cloth measuring 42cm × 34.5cm (16¹⁄₂in × 13¹⁄₂in):

*50cm × 44cm (20in × 17¹⁄₂in) of ivory,
27-count Linda fabric
Stranded embroidery cotton in the colours given
in the appropriate panel
No24 tapestry needle
Matching sewing thread*

●

THE EMBROIDERY

Take the fabric to be used for the embroidery and prepare it as described on page 4; find the centre by folding, and mark the horizontal and vertical centre lines with basting stitches in a light-coloured thread. Set the fabric in a frame and count out from the centre to start stitching at a point convenient to you.

Complete the cross stitching first, using two strands of thread in the needle; take each stitch over two strands of fabric in each direction and make sure that all top stitches run in the same direction. Continue with the backstitching, using one strand of dark brown thread in the needle to outline the body of the cow.

Remove the embroidery from the frame. Gently handwash the finished piece, if necessary, and lightly press with a steam iron on the wrong side.

FINISHING THE TRAY CLOTH

Keeping the embroidery centred, trim the cloth to measure 44.5cm × 37cm (17¹⁄₂in × 14¹⁄₂in). Using matching thread, neaten the raw edges with machine zigzag, then turn under a 12mm (¹⁄₂in) hem and machine around all sides.

For an alternative, more traditional finish, you might choose to finish the edges with a fringe, held with hemstitching. For this you will need one skein of stranded cotton, to match the fabric. Trim the cloth, as above, then remove a thread of fabric at the hemline, 12mm (¹⁄₂in) in from the raw edge. Using two strands of cotton in the needle, and taking each stitch around either three or four threads of the fabric, hemstitch around the tray cloth, along the

hemline, as shown below. When you have finished, remove the weft threads below the hemstitching, to make a fringe.

HEMSTITCH

Bring the needle out on the right side, two threads below the drawn-thread line. Working from the left to right, pick up threads, as shown in the diagram. Bring the needle out again and insert it behind the fabric, to emerge two threads down, ready to make the next stitch. Before inserting the needle, pull the thread tight, so that the bound threads form a neat group.

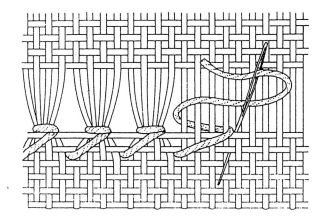

COW AND CALF ▶	ANCHOR	DMC	MADEIRA
⊢ Sand	942	738	2013
∷ Light golden brown	1045	437	2012
⊤ Rich brown	310	434	2009
⊣ Grey	8581	646	1812
⊻ Grass green	265	471	1501
⊠ Purple	97	209	0803
· White	1	White	White
❘ Dark sand	943	436	2011
☐ Golden brown	1046	435	2010
■ Dark brown	382	3371	2004
⊞ Pink	893	225	0814
▪ Blue	176	809	0909
▦ Dark green	268	580	1608

Note: backstitch around the cow and calf in dark brown.

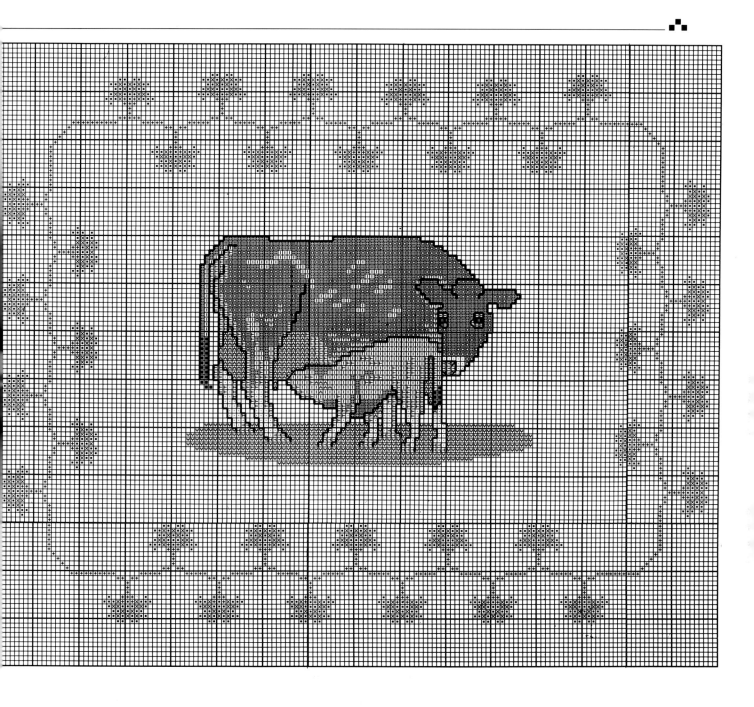

Cockerel
Cushion

This proud fellow – a true king of
the farmyard – is richly designed,
with threads of different textures
on a subtle peach background.
Here, he has been made into a
cushion cover, but he could be
framed as a picture.

COCKEREL CUSHION

YOU WILL NEED

For the *Cockerel* cushion, measuring
37cm (14½in) square, with a design area of
25.5cm (10in) square:

47cm (18½in) of peach, 25-count Lugano fabric
Stranded embroidery cotton in the colours given
in the panel
No24 tapestry needle
39.5cm (15½in) square of peach fabric,
for backing
2.3m (2½yds) of matching peach No2 piping cord
Matching sewing thread
38cm (15in) square cushion pad

*NOTE: Anchor Marlitt polyester threads were used
here to give a slight contrast in texture; the Madeira,
Decora threads are also polyester; there is no DMC
equivalent, though you might mix the stranded
cottons suggested with blending filaments for a
similar effect.*

•

THE EMBROIDERY

Prepare the fabric as described on page 4; find the
centre by folding, and mark the horizontal and
vertical centre lines with basting stitches in a light-
coloured thread. Set the fabric in a frame (see page
5) and count out from the centre to start stitching at
a point convenient to you.

Complete the cross stitching, using two strands of
the appropriate thread in the needle for all cross
stitches. Take all cross stitches over two threads of
fabric in each direction, and make sure that all top
stitches run in the same direction. Finish with the
backstitching, using one thread of stranded cotton
in the needle.

Take the finished embroidery from the frame
and remove any basting stitches. Wash if necessary,
then press lightly on the wrong side, using a steam
iron.

MAKING THE COVER

Keeping the embroidery centred, trim the fabric to
measure 39.5cm (15½in) square. With right sides
together and taking a 12mm (½in) seam allowance,
machine stitch the backing fabric and the
embroidered front cover together, leaving a 32cm
(12½in) gap at one side. Trim across the seam
allowance at corners to remove excess fabric; neaten
raw edges, and turn the cover right side out.

Insert the cushion pad, and slipstitch the
opening, but still leave a small 2.5cm (1in) opening.
Slipstitch piping cord around the edge of the
cushion, inserting the ends into the remaining small
opening, then slipstitch the opening.

COCKEREL ▶		ANCHOR	DMC	MADEIRA
■	Black	403	310	Black
+	Bright yellow	291	444	0106
T	Orange	303	742	0114
⊢	Dark pink	11	350	0213
⊦	Light tan	1001	976	2302
▪	Tan	1004	920	0312
Ⅰ	Light purple	871	3042	0807
∷	Emerald green	209	912	1213
⅃	Rich emerald green	210	561	1206
·	White	1	White	White
⊠	Dark green	268	580	1608
□	Yellow	295	726	0100
⊥	Grass green	266	470	1502
⊣	Red	13	321	0510
⧄	Soft brown	349	301	2306
⊟	Dark purple	873	3740	0806
L	Pine	218	890	1314
◪	Dark bright green	1067 Marlitt	909	D1496
⊠	Rust	1003 Marlitt	943	D1495
⌐	Rich bright green	1066 Marlitt	3345	D1556
⌑	Dark green	853 Marlitt	319	D1570

Note: backstitch around beak and legs in pine, using one strand.

Leaping Lamb Picture Frame

These little lambs are gambolling among poppies. The whites and bright reds are brought to life by the sky blue background – a photograph of your loved ones will complete the design.

LEAPING LAMB
PICTURE FRAME

For the *Leaping Lamb* picture frame, with
an internal measurement of 24cm × 29cm
(9½in × 11½in), and a cut-out as specified below:

*36cm × 42cm (14in × 16½in) of pale blue,
14-count Aida fabric
Stranded embroidery cotton in the colours given
in the appropriate panel
No24 tapestry needle
Frame, as specified above
Mount to fit the frame, with a cut-out measuring
11.5cm × 16cm (4½in × 6¼in) or to display your
favourite photograph
Masking tape and clear fabric glue*

●

THE EMBROIDERY

Prepare the fabric as described on page 4; find
the centre by folding, and mark the horizontal and
vertical centre lines with basting stitches in a
light-coloured thread. Set the fabric in a frame and
count out from the centre to start stitching at a point
convenient to you.

Complete the cross stitching, using two strands of
thread in the needle and making sure that all top
stitches run in the same direction. Finish with the
backstitched outlines, using one strand of grey
thread in the needle.

Remove the embroidery from the frame. Gently
handwash the finished piece, if necessary, and
lightly press with a steam iron on the wrong side.

COMPLETING THE FRAME

Stretch and mount the embroidery over the
cardboard mount, mitring the corners and using
masking tape to hold the edges as explained on
page 6. Leaving a margin of 3cm (1¼in) on all sides,
cut away spare fabric from the centre of the mount.
Snip diagonally into the corners, then bring the
edges of the fabric to the back of the mount and

again secure with masking tape. To prevent fraying
and hold the fabric securely, put a dab of glue at the
back of the mount on the inner corners.

Tape the photograph in place behind the mount
and insert the mounted picture into the frame.
Finish assembling the frame according to the
manufacturer's instructions.

Back view of mount showing centre cut and
ready to be taped back.

LEAPING LAMB ▶	ANCHOR	DMC	MADEIRA
⊥ Ecru	387	Ecru	1908
▦ Grey	399	414	1801
T Yellow	295	726	0100
⊢ Bright green	267	3346	1407
⊞ Dark pink	11	350	0213
· White	1	White	White
∷ Pale pink	25	3689	0607
☐ Green	261	989	1401
■ Black	403	310	Black
▪ Red	13	321	0510

Note: backstitch around lambs in grey.

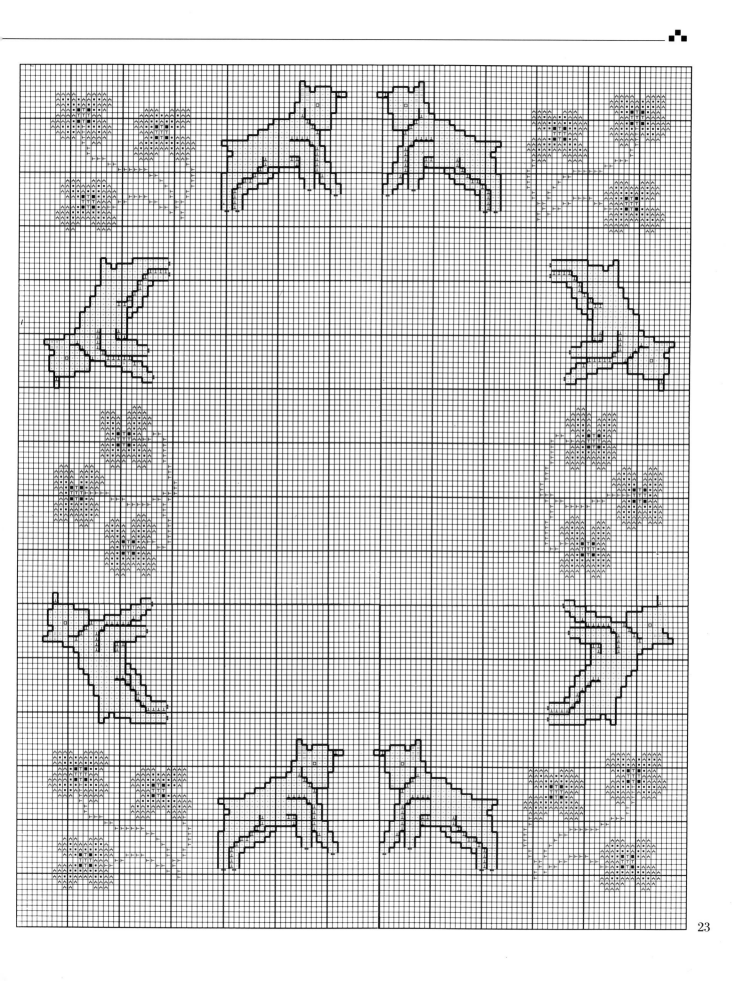

Hen Cot Cover

The snuggly soft fabric of this cot cover/shawl, which is decorated with a simple repeated pattern of bright brown hens, will keep baby warm and cosy. The hen motifs could also be used for pretty birthday cards.

HEN COT COVER

To make the cot cover, measuring
90cm × 75.5cm (35$\frac{1}{2}$in × 29$\frac{3}{4}$in) excluding
the fringe:

109cm × 94cm (43in × 37in) of Anne cloth
Stranded embroidery cotton in the colours given
in the panel
No24 tapestry needle
Matching sewing thread

NOTE: Anne cloth is a specially-produced evenweave
fabric, divided by bands of contrast weaving into
squares, suitable for cross-stitched motifs; for
suppliers see page 40.

•

THE EMBROIDERY

Refer to the diagram and position the motifs as
follows:
1 Hen facing to the right,
2 Sitting hen, facing right,
3 Sitting hen, facing left.
Mark the centre of each square that is to contain
a hen motif with horizontal and vertical lines of
basting stitches in a light-coloured thread. For each
motif, set the fabric in a hoop (see page 4) and count
out from the centre to start stitching at a point
convenient to you. To avoid marking the fabric, take
the fabric from the hoop at the end of each
embroidery session.

Complete the cross stitching, using three strands
of thread in the needle and making sure that all
top stitches run in the same direction. Finish the
standing hens by backstitching around the legs and
claws, using one strand of dark brown in the needle.

Remove the embroidery from the hoop. Gently
handwash the finished piece, if necessary, and lightly press with a steam iron on the wrong side.

FINISHING

Using matching sewing thread and a machine zigzag
stitch, sew along the outer of the two bold white lines
of Anne cloth, around the outside of the blank
squares, enclosing an area approximately 90cm ×
75.5cm (35$\frac{1}{2}$in × 29$\frac{3}{4}$in). Trim the cover to leave an
allowance of 4cm (1$\frac{1}{2}$in) beyond the zigzag stitching.
On each side, carefully remove parallel threads
back to the stitched line, and smooth out the
resulting fringe.

		1		
	2		3	
		1		
	2		3	

HENS ▲	ANCHOR	DMC	MADEIRA
■ Red	19	347	0407
+ Light rust	369	3776	2302
T Brown	370	400	2305
⊢ Dark brown	380	801	2007
⌐ Golden brown	1045	436	2011
▪ Straw	887	734	1610
✕ Black	403	310	Black
□ Rust	349	301	2306
⊥ Rich brown	357	300	2304
⊣ Pale gold	361	676	2208

Note: backstitch legs and claws in dark brown.

Farmyard Sampler

Combining tradition with modern design, this pretty little sampler really is the 'ABC' of the farm, the subtle sage green fabric complementing the bright colours. The motifs could be used on linen, greetings cards or children's clothes.

FARMYARD SAMPLER

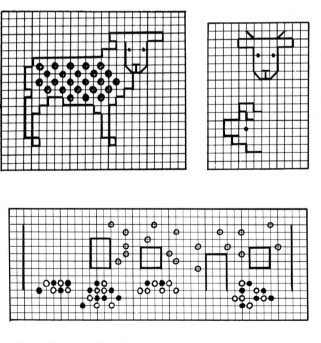

YOU WILL NEED

For the sampler, with a design area measuring
20cm × 23.5cm (8in × 9¹/₄in), here set in a frame
with an internal measurement of 31.5cm × 35.5cm
(12¹/₂in × 14in):

*44cm × 47cm (17¹/₂in × 18¹/₂in) of sage green,
14-count Aida fabric*
*Stranded embroidery cotton in the colours given
in the panel*
No24 tapestry needle
Frame, as specified above
Strong thread and cardboard, for mounting

●

THE EMBROIDERY

Prepare the fabric as described on page 4; find
the centre by folding, and mark the horizontal and
vertical centre lines with basting stitches in a light-
coloured thread. Set the fabric in a frame (see page
5) and count out from the centre to start stitching at
a point convenient to you.

Complete the cross stitching, using two strands of
thread in the needle and making sure that all top
stitches run in the same direction. Continue with the
backstitching, this time using one strand only for all
backstitching in dark grey and rich green, and two
strands for backstitching in fawn, pink, ecru and
black. Finish with french knots; the large knots that
make the flowers on the farmhouse and the fleecy
coats of the sheep are worked with two strands and
are indicated on the chart by circles, each enclosing
a graph intersection. The eyes of the pigs, sheep and
cows are also made with french knots, this time
worked with one strand only.

FINISHING

Remove the sampler from the frame. Gently
handwash the finished piece, if necessary, and
lightly press with a steam iron on the wrong side.
Stretch and mount the embroidery as explained on
page 6. Insert the mounted embroidery into the
frame, and assemble the frame according to the
manufacturer's instructions.

**Backstitch and
french knot details**

FARMYARD ▶ SAMPLER		ANCHOR	DMC	MADEIRA
■	Grey	399	414	1801
＋	Black	403	310	Black
T	Rich brown	358	433	2008
⊣	Pale brick	882	402	2307
▪	Pink	73	963	0608
ǀ	Medium pink	1017	316	0809
∷	Yellow green	255	907	1410
⌐	Yellow	295	726	1019
⊓	Rust	349	301	2306
·	White	1	White	White
⊠	Ecru	387	Ecru	1908
□	Brown	371	434	2009
⊢	Fawn	372	729	2209
⊣	Apple green	265	471	1501
⊠	Dark pink	1018	3726	0810
−	Rich green	257	905	1412
L	Blue	145	799	0910
⌐	Red	19	817	0211
	Dark grey*	400	317	1714
	Purple	110	209	0803

*Note: backstitch around the farmhouse walls, roof and windows,
and the pigs, sheep and cows in dark grey* (used for backstitch
only); backstitch the pig tails in pink, the sheep tails in ecru, the
cow tails in black, the hen legs and claws in fawn, and the stem of
the climbing rose in rich green. The french knots are shown on the
detail charts only.*

Farmhouse. The flowers in the farmhouse motif
are worked with two strands of cotton.
○ Yellow ◖ Ecru
● Red ⊕ Purple

Mallards Tea Cosy

Fresh white provides the perfect background for the wild irises and pond, on which swim a striking mallard and his mate. The scene is a restful design for the tea table, but could equally well be set into a small tray or framed as a picture.

MALLARDS TEA COSY

YOU WILL NEED

For the *Mallards* tea cosy, measuring
30.5cm × 24cm (12in × 9½in):

*40cm × 36cm (16in × 14in) of white,
14-count Aida fabric
36cm × 30.5cm (14in × 12in) of white,
Aida or similar fabric, for back of tea cosy
Two 36cm × 30.5cm (14in × 12in) pieces of white,
cotton fabric, for inner lining
Two 36cm × 30.5cm (14in × 12in) pieces of polyester
batting/wadding
Stranded embroidery cotton in the colours given
in the panel
No24 tapestry needle
1m (1¼yds) of No2 piping cord
Matching sewing thread*

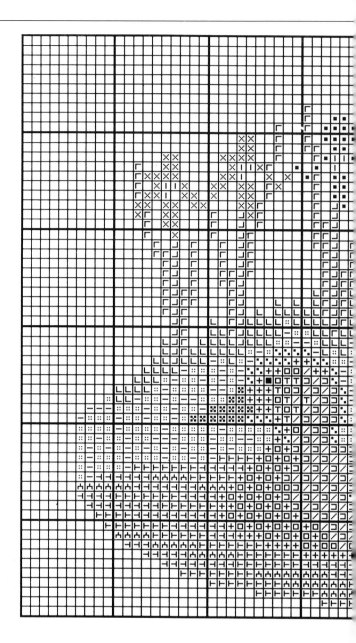

THE EMBROIDERY

Prepare the Aida fabric and stretch it in a frame as
explained on page 4; find the centre by folding, and
mark the horizontal and vertical centre lines with
basting stitches in a light-coloured thread. Set the
fabric in a frame and count out from the centre to
start stitching at a convenient point. Complete
the cross stitching, using two strands of thread in
the needle. Remove the embroidery from the
frame. Leaving the basting stitches in place, gently
handwash the finished piece, if necessary,
and press with a steam iron on the wrong side.

MAKING THE TEA COSY

Scale up the template for the tea cosy shape and
make a paper pattern. Using the basting stitches as
guidelines to make sure that the embroidery is
centred, draw the outline on the back of the Aida
fabric with a well-sharpened hard lead pencil. Cut
out, adding a 12mm (½in) seam allowance all around
the marked shape. Repeat with the backing fabric
and the two pieces of lining fabric. Cut two shapes
from batting/wadding, this time without adding the
seam allowance.

Remove the basting stitches from the
embroidered piece and, with right sides together and
taking a 12mm (½in) seam allowance, join the cosy
back and front together around the long curved
seam. For each lining section, lay the corresponding

batting/wadding piece on the wrong side, within
the marked outline, and machine stitch the two
together, making three vertical lines of stitches,
one up the centre, and one at each side, 10cm (4in)
from the centre line. With right sides together and
taking the 12mm (½in) seam allowance, join the
padded lining pieces together around the long
curved seam.

Turn the outer cover right side out and slipstitch
piping along the curved seam, from the lower raw
edge at one side to the lower raw edge at the other
side, making a loop at the top of the cosy. Bring the
lower, straight edge of the lining over, covering the
edge of batting/wadding, and turn under the lower
straight edge of the outer cover. Fit lining into outer
cover and slipstitch around bottom edge.

FOLDLINE

◄ **Tea cosy template**
Scale up by 165 per cent on a
photocopier and cut from folded paper.

MALLARDS ▲		ANCHOR	DMC	MADEIRA					
⅂	Dark sand	373	729	2209	•	White	1	White	White
+	Stone	831	3782	1907	⊠	Golden brown	365	780	2214
T	Greyish stone	392	642	1906	⊐	Pinky brown	832	3032	2002
�	Pale blue	130	799	0910	⊥	Straw	874	834	2204
⊣	Medium blue	977	826	1012	⊣	Bright blue	121	793	0906
■	Purple	109	210	0802	Y	Dark blue	922	930	1712
I	Yellow	297	725	0108	⊠	Dark purple	111	208	0804
∷	Olive green	844	581	1609	—	Pale olive green	842	772	1604
⅃	Bright green	266	3347	1408	L	Grass green	265	471	1501
⅂	Blue green	876	503	1702	Γ	Rich green	267	3346	1407
■	Black	403	310	Black	⊏	Pine green	878	561	1205
U	Bright brown	357	975	2302	⠔	Dark brown	889	3790	2106
╱	Dull brown	898	370	2112	◢	Very dark brown	382	3371	2004

Baby's Gift Set

The perfect gift for a young mother, this lovely set of two bibs and a towel features a donkey, a duck, and three lively pigs. These small motifs are relatively quickly embroidered, and could be stitched by a child.

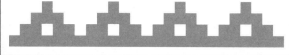

BABY'S GIFT SET

YOU WILL NEED

For the *Three Little Pigs* towel, measuring
46cm × 29cm (18in × 11½in), with a design area
measuring 25.5cm × 4cm (10in × 1½in) or
for the bibs, each measuring approximately
18.5cm × 15cm (7¼in × 6in), with a design area
measuring 6.5cm × 5cm (2½in × 2in), **Duck**, and
5cm × 4.5cm (2in × 1¾in), *Donkey*:

Stranded embroidery cotton in the colours given
in the appropriate panel
No24 tapestry needle
Chosen item (for suppliers, see page 40)
Strong thread to match the Aida Band (towel only)

NOTE: the towel already has the lace-edged Aida
band attached to it; if you wish to add embroidery
to an ordinary towel, you can purchase Aida band
from specialist suppliers (see page 40) and attach it
to the towel once you have decorated it with your
chosen motif.

•

THE EMBROIDERY

There is no need to use a hoop or frame for these
small items. For the bibs, decide where you intend
to position your motif and start stitching from
the centre outwards, using two strands of thread
in the needle for cross stitching and one for
backstitching.

The Aida band on the towel is attached on three
sides, leaving one long edge free so that you can
hold the band apart from the towel when cross
stitching. Mark the horizontal and vertical centre
lines of the towel with lines of basting stitches in a
light-coloured thread, and stitch from the centre,
again using two strands of thread in the needle for
cross stitches and one strand for backstitching.
Leave six Aida blocks between pigs.

FINISHING THE TOWEL

When you have finished embroidering the Aida
band, slip stitch the lower edge of the Aida band to
the towel, using matching thread and stitching along
the join between the Aida band and the lace trim.

THREE LITTLE PIGS ▼	ANCHOR	DMC	MADEIRA
■ Dark pink	895	223	0812
+ Blue	146	799	0911
▪ Pink	894	224	0813
☒ Grey	8581	646	1812
Dark grey*	400	317	1714

Note: backstitch around pigs in dark grey* (used for backstitching only).

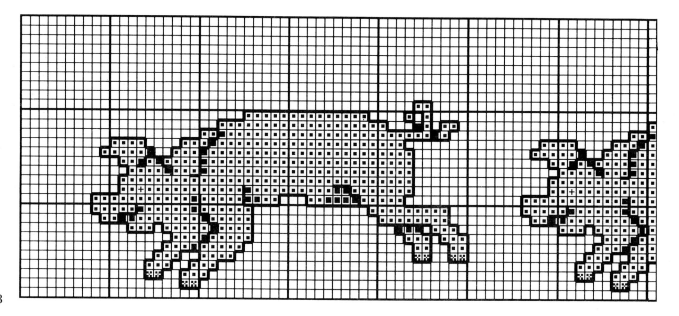

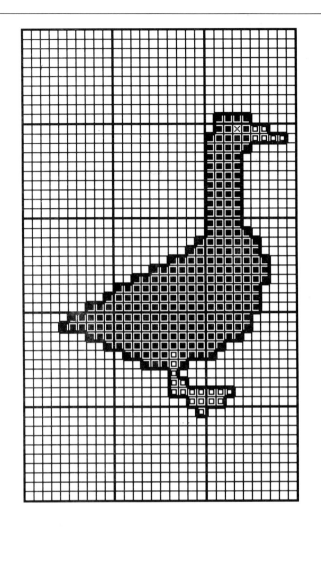

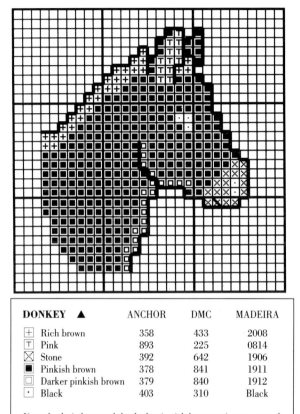

DUCK ◄	ANCHOR	DMC	MADEIRA
☐ Pink	894	224	0813
■ White	1	White	White
⊠ Blue	920	932	1710

Note: backstitch around the duck in blue, using one strand of thread in the needle.

DONKEY ▲	ANCHOR	DMC	MADEIRA
⊞ Rich brown	358	433	2008
T Pink	893	225	0814
⊠ Stone	392	642	1906
■ Pinkish brown	378	841	1911
☐ Darker pinkish brown	379	840	1912
· Black	403	310	Black

Note: backstitch around the donkey in rich brown, using one strand of thread in the needle.

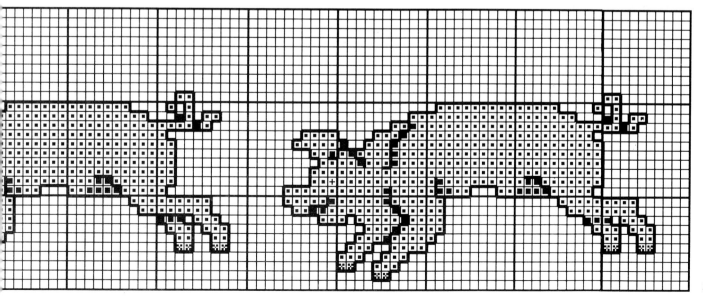

ACKNOWLEDGEMENTS

My thanks to Coats Patons Crafts, who kindly supplied the Anchor threads which were used throughout this book, and to DMC, who supplied the Zweigart fabrics.

Special thanks are also due to Alan Jones, picture framer, of 26 Chandos Road, Redland, Bristol, for his help in mounting and framing projects in this book.

SUPPLIERS

The towel and bibs on page 36 are available from:
Crafty Ideas
The Willows
1 Cassington Road
Eynsham
Oxon OX18 1LF
Telephone (01865) 880086

The following mail order company has supplied some of the basic items needed for making up the projects in this book:

Framecraft Miniatures Limited
372/376 Summer Lane
Hockley
Birmingham, B19 3QA
England
Telephone: (0121) 359 4442

Addresses for Framecraft stockists worldwide
Ireland Needlecraft Pty Ltd
2-4 Keppel Drive
Hallam, Victoria 3803
Australia

Danish Art Needlework
PO Box 442, Lethbridge
Alberta T1J 3Z1
Canada

Sanyei Imports
PO Box 5, Hashima Shi
Gifu 501-62
Japan

The Embroidery Shop
286 Queen Street
Masterton
New Zealand

Anne Brinkley Designs Inc.
246 Walnut Street
Newton
Mass. 02160
USA

S A Threads and Cottons Ltd.
43 Somerset Road
Cape Town
South Africa

For information on your nearest stockist of embroidery cotton, contact the following:

DMC (also distributors of Zweigart fabrics)
UK
DMC Creative World Limited
62 Pullman Road
Wigston
Leicester, LE8 2DY
Telephone: 01162 811040

USA
The DMC Corporation
Port Kearney Bld.
10 South Kearney
N.J. 07032-0650
Telephone: 201 589 0606

AUSTRALIA
DMC Needlecraft Pty
P.O. Box 317
Earlswood 2206
NSW 2204
Telephone: 02599 3088

COATS AND ANCHOR
UK
Coats Patons Crafts
McMullen Road
Darlington
Co. Durham DL1 1YQ
Telephone: 01325 381010

USA
Coats & Clark
P.O. Box 27067
Dept CO1
Greenville SC 29616
Telephone: 803 234 0103

AUSTRALIA
Coats Patons Crafts
Thistle Steet
Launceston
Tasmania 7250
Telephone: 00344 4222

MADEIRA
UK
Madeira Threads (UK) Limited
Thirsk Industrial Park
York Road, Thirsk
N. Yorkshire, YO7 3BX
Telephone: 01845 524880

USA
Madeira Marketing Limited
600 East 9th Street
Michigan City
IN 46360
Telephone: 219 873 1000

AUSTRALIA
Penguin Threads Pty Limited
25-27 Izett Street
Prahran
Victoria 3181
Telephone: 03529 4400